Articulations for Keeping the Light In

barbican young poets

**edited by Rachel Long
& Jacob Sam-La Rose**

flipped eye publishing
London

Articulations for Keeping the Light In
Barbican Young Poets 2022

First published by flipped eye publishing © 2022
Copyright © 2022, Barbican Centre
Cover Design © Petraski, 2022 | @petraski on www.twitter.com
Author Images © Betty Laura Zapata | www.bettylaurazapata.com;
Christy Ku | www.christyku.co.uk; Robert Taylor | www.taylor-photo.co.uk

This book is typeset in Trajan Pro and Palatino Linotype.

flipped eye publishing
www.flippedeye.net

ISBN-13: 978-1-905233-79-3

LOTTERY FUNDED
Supported using public funding by
ARTS COUNCIL ENGLAND

ARTICULATIONS FOR KEEPING THE LIGHT IN

Barbican Young Poets
2022

barbican

Barbican Creative Learning

Barbican Creative Learning pioneers new models for creative and cultural learning across the art forms. Our mission, **Creative Skills for Life**, underpins all aspects of our work and approach in the design and delivery of meaningful and impactful learning experiences across three strategic areas:

- **Education**: supporting creativity in the classroom through arts-based learning programmes and tailored partnerships with schools and specialist educational settings, locally and nationally
- **Employability**: producing talent development programmes, and higher education and career pathways, with and for people looking to work within the creative industries
- **Enrichment**: producing participatory programmes, and collaborating with charity and community organisations, to create meaningful arts experiences that support the wellbeing of people of all ages and backgrounds

In 2020/21, we delivered 20 digital and physical programmes with over 200 partners, engaging 2,400 participants, and reaching an audience of more than 50,000. In order to achieve this, we build partnerships with teachers, artists, young people, schools, and community organisations locally, nationally, and internationally. At the heart of our work and practice is a commitment to **people, partnership,** and **place.**

Articulations for Keeping the Light In

Barbican Young Poets 2022

Foreword

Barbican Creative Learning is delighted to welcome you to the Barbican Young Poets Anthology 2022; a poetry anthology that showcases the work of our immensely talented community of young artists.

At Barbican Creative Learning we work alongside young people, supporting them to develop their creative skills and raise their confidence and self-esteem. The work you read inside this anthology has been created by emerging poets aged 18-30, living locally in London and further afield across the country, who have been working together as part of a community of young poets for the past six months, under the inspired guidance of renowned poets and educators, Jacob Sam-La Rose and Rachel Long.

Barbican Young Poets come together for fortnightly workshops at the Barbican, working with Jacob and Rachel to explore a diverse range of poetic genres, styles, and themes to push their developing voices in new directions. The poets study both the craft of writing, and the power of performing their material live. They are encouraged to discover what is unique about their own artistic voice, supporting and challenging each other as peers and evolving together as part of a community of young artists.

It has been two years since we last published an anthology, which, for ten years prior, had been an annual event. In that hiatus sits the COVID-19 pandemic, and all that has meant to the communities of young people, artists, and partners that we collaborate with here at the Barbican. The work of Barbican Young Poets has been for some years now an embodiment of zeitgeist for the Barbican; expressions of thoughts and ideas that speak to particular moments in culture. On reading these pieces, you learn about that moment in time, just as you learn about what it means for the poet writing the piece. It feels vitally important, in these times of unprecedented uncertainty and, for many in the world, hardship, to provide space in the Barbican for young artists with so much to say to come together.

We are thrilled this year to be working in partnership with flipped eye publishing to bring the work of our young poets to meet professional poetry publishing. We are sure that this platform will broaden the readership of our young artists and extend the reach of their poetry.

On behalf of this year's cohort, and the Creative Learning staff who produce the programme, I would like to thank Jacob and Rachel for all that they do to make Barbican Young Poets a programme to be proud of. The Barbican has learnt much from the partnership with Jacob through Barbican Young Poets; like the best collaborations, it yields something new with each passing year.

It is a delight and a privilege to work with such a talented group of young people, and we hope you are inspired by the work collected here in their anthology.

Lauren Monaghan-Pisano
Senior Producer
Barbican Creative Learning

Introduction

I recently had the occasion to deliver a short speech about the significance of Barbican Young Poets for a gathering of esteemed stakeholders and potential supporters. Fortuitously, as I was gathering my thoughts for that speech, a couple of old BYPs got back in touch, completely unbidden, to let me know how they were doing. One of them is now an ophthalmologist and parent (among other things); the other, a research lecturer for a European arts school. Hearing from both of them, about their joys and successes, and where and how they've landed in roles and lives that fit them so completely, I came to consider the "mission" that drives the work we've done through this programme over the years.

In speaking of Barbican Young Poets, I often talk about community, of what a community of practice can look like, a community established not only on a deep investment in the development of creative practice but also a firm foundation of care for its members. And it occurs to me that the mission (if you'll forgive me the use of such grandiose language) is more than that. We celebrate and strive for whatever we might define as best in poetry and our respective visions of poetry — yes. We do what we can to construct a space in which our constituents feel safe enough to experiment, take risks and share aspects of themselves they might otherwise keep under wraps — yes. But beyond all those key considerations, through our annual series of meetings, workshops, prompts, challenges, off-topic tangents, after-session conversations, shared Google documents for feedback, group WhatsApp exchanges and all the other countless ways in which we interact, we construct experiences that can impact, inform or expand the possibilities for the lives of the people we hold space for. Regardless of whether those lives are lived out as "professional" poets, writers, performers, or any of the other shapes those lives might take.

Those impacts and experiences don't just come about through me and all my method-in-madness facilitation, planning and breaking plans in favour of whatever's present, immediate and responsive to our poets' needs in the moment. It's not just about the collaboration between myself and Rachel Long, to whom I'm perennially indebted for continuing to help chart a meaningful path through all of the things we could offer each year. It's not even about the way we work together with Lauren Brown (who, as Creative Learning Producer for Theatre, Dance and Poetry, has made the hard job of herding poets seem effortless with inimitable grace). It's how we all, poets and participants included, come together to hold these experiences for each other.

The past few years have not been easy for many of us. There was no core 20-21 Barbican Young Poets programme, our first hiatus in over a decade's worth of programme delivery. Returning this year, we've had to learn (again, like so many others) how to do what we do in ever more accessible ways (I give thanks and praise for Simon Morgan and Rikky Onefeli for their unfailing support in all things streamed and technological). After all these years, we are all still learning. And there's something exciting about that. While there's always more to be done, if the work anthologised here can provide any indication or measure, we're still on mission, and I don't think we're doing too badly at all.

Jacob Sam-La Rose
Artistic Director and Lead Facilitator
Barbican Young Poets

Oshanti Ahmed

Did You Release Termites

when you slept with me?   *Sneaky*
Do you understand how they work?   No   eyes
to see what of me is good flesh   They eat
aimlessly   I feel a constant   tunnelling   even
when I'm alone   They demand negative space
just to exist   Do you know how it feels to be so
full and empty at the same time?   All my
capillaries just a fresh opportunity   They are
replacing my eggs for their own   When there are
a thousand things living in   you   become   so
so   *needy*   I feel sorry for the next person who
wants me   They'll be sitting horrified when I let
them in bed now every time   it feels like
immolation   Now   now   now   *How
embarrassing*   I won't be able to hear anyone
say that they love me over the tiny insect teeth
feasting on   I put my ears between my thighs   I
hear   my body bickering   resentment towards
me

Esme Allman

Uncle Theodore

I have an uncle. Soft-spoken.
Star Wars fan. Can be found

laser focused, crooning
the *ggzz* sound of his lightsaber.

I didn't see him for years. Dad told me
he'd gone missing, though to where

Dad wouldn't say. He likes the moon
and the planets. If he could, he'd go.

That started the rumour about him
coming to the door in a babydoll.

Blue negligée. A flitting giggle
identifiable by only the women

in my family. Once, on the way
to Grandma's, I bumped into him

on her road. Cowed against licks of wind
I slackened, squinting for her worn

cerulean door. Thought before I knew
I was sure – that's Uncle Theo. He didn't

register me. *Uncle Theo,* I called.
Startle, then recognition, his face bursting

into doughy joy. He said I looked wonderful
like I should be reporting on the news.

mandisa apena

night-time travel

we live in the stillness before the waning sun
and it is absolute symphony.
we wait for the mist and the moon springing beneath it
which dresses our skin in sleep.
our bodies are ripened in their smooth sweaty glaze.
this is when the hand of the sky plucks me
summoned, floating,
and places me back in the blue hollow of a tree
where i swim low but flinch from the darkening bottom
and secrets of the root. then; i was outside a temple
cradled inside a mile-wide pit. everything carved of the earth itself.
led there by a copper man so touched by knowledge
that it sang from inside out, and all his people
and why are we all standing here? dreaming
that i was to warn a civilisation living under the earth
in all their huddled love and purple cloth
that the white people were coming
and you should not trust them.
on another night, i stood beside myself
and had to choose between two doors.
you'd never understand. i had to make that decision.
i'm learning fast; met the self just beneath the surface
who watches time - raw and bare and enormous –
live a thousand languid summers
over the trudge of my gorgeous elaborate meat.

the witness

i am a quiet buzz
drawn towards the sticky
of your crevices.
fixated, but batted away
by one of the three women
who suspire as they settle
and resettle on your shoulders.
they are somehow
all your mother.
they are preparing
wedding speeches,
are knotting fate to your scalp
with their talons.
your cornrows
hum in prayer.
these mothers are wardens
of your heart, so you confide
about his eyes:
unfamiliar... sharp.
i dive for your sweetness again,
am swatted,
three times,
then escape and i'm forgotten
on the drag of your hem.
behind your dishwater dress
you have pinched
from the sky,
i track the sun in my thousand-vision.
watch a thousand trembling yous,
all pinching your way to the altar,

where he is gorgeous
and unsettling.
you stand opposite him,
and say nothing.
when it is time to exchange vows,
you say nothing.
keep level with his eyes.
i can feel your hope for mercy
under his gaze.
i know that, too. amen.
i know that, too.
i've got my fly's eye view.
zig zagging the air behind you
into your blue car,
becoming trapped.
hammering my face
into the cold glassy
landscape of out.
when we arrive,
i'm let out like a
gasp, we all are.
you, who i'm driven up behind,
down a path paved
by dead ambrosia bushes.
still mad by your sweat.
inside your house
there is a scythe on the table,
which he grabs,
and brings to your throat,
the skin sudden beneath it,
your each exhale
an apology. *sorry, i'm sorry.*

Rachel Cleverly

Cutting

Unsurprisingly,
in turn, we had both been cut.
Him first (minutely)

now me (much too much).
With the knife he started to
slice. My nail was stuck

straight up, hanging on
its hinge, unnecessary.
I had been dicing

onions. Then I was
slicing skin. A lip of nail
slid under the blade

as the onions rolled,
skinless, yet gratingly whole.
I'd ruined dinner.

He grabbed back the knife,
then once we finished eating
I was left alone

with the washing up.
I stacked spoons, forks, bowls and cups.
The knife went into

the sink. I ran the
sponge from handle to tip. Nail
throbbed. The bubbles split.

The Patient

A roaring sneeze started it; the patient could think of nothing except her nose.
'If you collected colds like you do mental illnesses,' said the GP, 'you'd be dead by now.'
This didn't help the patient feel any better. Her family had a history of agoraphobia –
they'd lived long and limited lives. The GP thought the patient obsessed
over consequence, leaving her few freedoms in the present. 'Even doctors get sick and die,'
said the GP. The patient felt her condition worsen, noticed a new violence in her sneezes.

The patient left her house less, switching to phone appointments when the sneezes
began to overwhelm. #8 in the hold queue, she leant on the window, pushed her nose
against the glass. #6, she saw her neighbour with a dog on the grass. They would die
soon too. #5, another sneeze, the dog paused, leg raised, and crossed the lawn she now
refused to cross herself. #4, the dog hunted the noise, increasingly obsessed
with it. #3: the patient erased her Google search *Can you treat agoraphobia*

at home? and found the sneeze sound echoed the pained howl of a hound Agoraphobia
didn't exist for the neighbour's dog – he advanced as the patient, plagued by sneezes,
reached #2 in the queue. #1, the call clicked through. The dog, obsessed
with the sound, strained against his owner, pressed his flaring, mud-coated black nose
against the window. Hearing the patient's mucus coated greeting, the GP hung up. Now
(the patient realised), today, tomorrow, next week – she'd be alone when it was time to die.

Three days later the patient's mail order puppy arrived. She'd made sure he wouldn't die
before her – he'd passed his medical examinations and roamed free of agoraphobia.
The patient called him Epidemic – Mick, for short. The first week was fine. Now
Mick had garden access and regular park trips, albeit punctuated by the patient's sneezes.
Day seven, he protested his limits by shitting on the neighbour's lawn in front of her nose.
The patient suspected Mick didn't prioritise safety over stimulation, and grew obsessed

with researching his internal life online. She found that canines are obsessed
with the present. Though she'd been concerned with how and when she might die,

a dog has little awareness of time; they can't travel across moments in their mind, their nose doesn't know how to find order in memory. Stuck in the present, the patient's agoraphobia now confined Mick to the lawn. She felt sorry for him – Mick had always taken her sneezes seriously. When the patient gave him an extra treat Mick barked 'Now! Now! Now!'

His understanding of time was limited, but his stomach was not. He'd now grown crafty, taught himself to crack open cupboards and drawers. He was obsessed with stealing and eating. On his last day Mick thought the patient distracted by sneezes. She caught him, mid-massacring a bar of Galaxy and four Creme Eggs. He was going to die. He needed a vet. The patient felt the pull of his life, and the press of agoraphobia. She wrestled him under her arm, pushed his chain collar to click around his writhing nose.

Despite a round of sneezes the patient opened the door, holding tight. But 'now!' thought Mick, taking a bite of her nose. He wriggled out from her arms. Obsessed with escape and so happy he could die, Mick passed the fence, fleeing.

Courtney Conrad

Extradition of Drug Lord Dudus Coke: Barbican Girl Dash Weh Tivoli Boy

Dudus / breath-taker of dutty yutes / preying on likkle girls' cellphones and chochos / he pretzels politicians' arms / so fathers can tief light to keep stoves on / his cash lines the bras of single mothers / who send their sons to your school / with their A*s / waves and clarks shoes / you copy their homework / follow them into bathroom stalls / slick bun bobbing in front of khaki zipper /

prime minister bruce golding / approves Dudus' extradition / your principal's intercom interrupts lunchtime / year group becomes a herd of whispers / shuffling to collect bags / ears cock for loose lips on staff walkie talkies / everyone sprints to their drivers / your boy / shoves himself into a tivoli chi-chi bus / that mounts sidewalks to get him home / meanwhile / your barbican prado / cruises to water polo training /

at training / with every other stroke you glance at the plumes of smoke / from tivoli / in the distance / police helicopters chopping your coach's commands / three missed calls from your boy / usually you're the needy one / you listen to his voicemail when you get home / *jah know mi nuh know if me and mi family dem a guh mek it / if mi dead / and dem seh mi did shoot afta di police / a lie dem a tell /*

meanwhile / in the name of President Dudus / tivoli gunmen buss shot after shot / not even a spot check for granny-less verandas / scrap vehicles and gas cylinders block cherry stain streets / your boy's eardrums grind like pimento / his little sister and brother's squeals stow in their kitchen cupboards / from his bedroom window he prees three of his bredrins plead the blood of jesus as they sit in their own / pooling / while rumours have it / underground / Dudus is a sewer rat / wearing a stiff wig for disguise /

the next day / prime minister calls for a state of emergency for tivoli / you neither adjust / nor die / but your boy vanishes / for a while / you ramp next to his empty desk / ask about his whereabouts / but not enough / in the tivoli community / mothers are graduating from sniffing foreheads / green armpits / to heaving at compost flesh / top lips marrying snotty nose-tips / single beds / open caskets

Mi Hope Yuh Know Fi Teach Like Yuh Know Fi Prey

I erase my test scores with extracurricular activities.
My teacher insists I do tutoring with her.
Yuh a troublemaker; I was bush-fucking at your age.
She parts her legs until I see no underwear.
I add colour back to my face staring at a box of crayons.
My teeth sharpen my pencil, she snatches and slips one
in between her cleavage. *Guh fi it.* My tight fist enters.
She moves furniture behind the door and I can tell
she lifts and pushes the sofa and fridge at home.
I fail the class worse than before.

*

For the entire season, she volunteers
as my after-school club monitor, rubbing sunblock
into my goal post shoulders and concrete thighs.
Sailing the ball in her direction for a wet decapitation.
Gulping vodka like Gatorade. Even for morning training.

*

Migrating in a month, she stalks me at my mother's company.
Takes her final sighting and feel while exchanging her receipt.
Nuh forget mi, come back with an accent.

*

This role-play feels familiar.
I remember her.
I speak about her for the first time
standing up for her as she taught me.
My partner's worry puts lust in detention
and asks, *would you be okay with it if it happens to our daughter?*

Bella Cox

Cake

Make a comb of your fingers, make sand of my hair, let's gather something sweet and dreaming into existence. Your blue paint body lying sticky next to mine. An acrylic sky. Hey don't go —

Stay. With all that tacky permanent brilliance, stay. Push the blade of your pocket knife tongue back inside the flesh of your pocket cheek. Congeal in our sweet-smelling potential — no, I know it's not optimal.

Solid sulphur merging with aching blue turns to mould. Another chest, another lover's shack. React. Barefoot in the darkness, I know you howled at your moon-eyed face in the mirror the night you found out. Altered me into a bone of lamb, revenge for all that internal mutilation. Left that gnawing slab of betrayal still sizzling in our hot bed of —

Vanilla —

Bring that with the comb. Bathe with me. Make amateur priests of our hands. Scented forgiveness and touch. Mould us back into sweetness.

Fall again with me, heavy but deft, two willing eggs into sand-like flour. Melt into soft again. Gentle, submissive, butter. Forget we ever smelt the mercaptan.

Not Marble

Blackout poem from Alias Grace *by Margaret Atwood*

A surgeon should be human

Deliberately   and delicately   steady

Suffering
                        the knife.

Men and women   are not marble.

They   become noisy   and leaky.

mysteries   to be   revealed

Both material   and ethereal

A thousand   shadowy bones

Scattered   like

                        angels.

Geraint Ellis

Cruciverbalism
(n.) presenting choice, through words

INSTRUCTIONS

Complete this crossword to create your poem. Know there is more than one solution.

OR

Do not complete this crossword. Perhaps your poem is content without it.

ACROSS

5 Possessive adjective (3)

8 Moving, delicately – due to breath, or wind? (10)

11 Paradise (4)

14 The foundations of an unexpected event (11)

15 Aromatic herb of the flowering Apiaceae family (7)

16 Skin irritation due to exposure to discomfort, or heat (7)

18 A prize to be taken (5)

19 Channel of water (5)

20 Belonging to one of your parents, within a nuclear family (7)

21 Mathematical process; two parts of an equation, at one stage apart, or, together (8)

22 Gradual development, through education or action (7)

23 Unfolding of events, as an individual hoped (8)

24 Fish, commonplace to marine waters of British, Atlantic and Baltic seas (6)

DOWN

1 French city, famed for arched masonry bridge (7)

2 Preparation, kitchen process on, say, root vegetables (7)

3 Cephalic or cerebral pain, causing loss of focus and attention (8)

4 Places for prayers to be answered, with offerings of coins (9)

5 Obscured (6)

6 Small, roundish juicy fruit, commonly used in jam or a fool (10)

7 Force that leads individuals, places and states to take actions and hold beliefs (9)

9 An abandoned or marooned person (8)

10 Moving, with purpose, or not (8)

12 Evening meal (6)

13 Will you play a crossword fast or slow? (7)

16 A frozen dessert (6)

17 Green vegetable, commonly served as a side (4)

The **9d** crossword
suspended in lapsed sentence
told how this stranger had **22a**, or was born, to draw **5a** 'S',
the light to heavy press of pen
a flow from hesitancy to confidence.
A reflection of a childhood preference for bashful silence, **5d** behind **20a** legs,
and a small fist reaching out for the **18a** –
cold soft scoop –
6d 16d
to break the **3d** daze
of a scorched afternoon spent in **1d,**
the maddening congregations round the **4d** thronging, jostling for baptism,
rather than shaded by the linden
bent to hear the susurrus of a **19a**

– a place you thought of as… **11a**.
It tells of **13d**
7d you,
and **21a** us –
how we use our time to chase a perfection that was ever intended,
answers given without judgement,
an alternative absent, forgotten.
Later, **10d** through the supermarket aisles,
the rain slick footprints you left led to a screwed-up shopping list
8a in your basket –
14a as though it were **23a**…
Reading it
would recreate your **12d**
fried **24a**, **2d** potato
and **15a** sauce with **17d** –
a peach for afters,
velvet flesh **16a** pink,
pressed against the lips.

Flotsam, Jetsam, Lagan, Wreck

Under a parasol in Olonzac
you read that a luthier has carved a violin
from Shackleton's floorboards
and that an expedition is searching for
the wreck of the Endurance.
I lick my finger to retrieve croissant flakes.
Perhaps they'll carve an orchestra from the skeleton
when it's lifted –
cellos cut from the deck,
violas from its heart.
We cycle out to the Lac de Jouarres
and dive in to search for lagan.
We cycle back as night falls.
You shout over your shoulder
that if you were carved into an instrument
it'd be a glockenspiel.
I lean back – the warm Marin dries my calves –
and stalk the sky for Polaris
but the only star is at your back wheel;
the lighthouse that charts my course.

Abena Essah

The Year of Return

In 1962, fifth year of Ghana's birth,
two MPs fail to assassinate President Kwame Nkrumah who
shouts "Long live African independence!" Kojo Besia stay in hiding,

whilst Grandmother stands still, lengthy, sturdy. Beehive combed
and poofy, holding my mother in a diaper, all bulging eyes.
The photographer will lift a lever and no one will smile to capture
the grace of the matriarch. This is how loving is made.

In the Year of Return, "Proper Ghanaian Family Values" brew
as thousands flood back through the gates in Accra

and I clutch the same grainy photo of my mothers,
sorrel creases dancing along the skin and dress of Grandmother.
Heavy nappy, Mother's eyes are still as alert, fixed on me. Her little hands
begin to shift, clamber out of the sea of yellowing grey,
until she is wailing in my arms.

I once clambered out of the warm blueness of her womb
when she grew to grow me. I sing, to my baby mother now, the song
that she would sing to me. *Baby little girl don't cry. Baby little girl
don't cry. I love you, you love me. Baby little girl don't cry.*
Mother your mother. This is how the matriarch is born.

What would she think if she knew? That I no longer assign
with the girl in these lyrics. That my body is more water than skin.
The song calms her and with paper filled mouth, she whimpers
What if my mother can't always hold me?
She will, I say.
And all at once every cardboard box full of her every iteration

throughout the years pulls off the shelves, albums ramming open.
The whole storeroom, a tornado of strained marriages,
teenage grins demanding not to be forgotten.

A thousand miles away, President Nana Akufo-Addo announces a bill,
for the social death of me, of my people,

whilst Grandmother lays crumpled in a hospital bed. Mother mirrors her,
on the couch in London, phone line pressed to her ears to keep track
of catheter beeps and groans. This is what the matriarch feels like.
My infant Mother's bulged eyes come in to meet her present and climbs
into my arms. *What if mother can't always hold me?*
both the grey and brown skinned mother begin wailing and I hold them both.

In the winter 2016 corruption is over,
Nana Akufo is president elect and swears by Freedom and Justice,

I fold myself through a crack in the door, my grey infant mother in hand.
The Mother that raised me sits on the edge of her husband's bed –
with her mother's borrowed perseverance – waiting for me block her body
from smothering. I hold her and her past in my arms once more
baby little girl don't cry, baby little girl don't cry.
Father will grunt and take what he needs when I finally leave.

Years later, there will be marches in the streets of London, the blood
in the flag outside the Ghana High Commission will stain the windows
and I will hold a mic to my mouth to try and halt time,
death, to halt history for my people

when I come home, Grandmother will see me on FaceTime,
and stay focused on my shaved head, Mother will egg her on
and I will mourn the matriarch that I could not quite fold my body into.

In our 64th year of independence,
21 people will be detained for unlawful homosexual carnal acts in my Ghana,

and my mother will shout in my face when she learns of my boyhood.
This is how the matriarch is preserved.

An ocean away, I am in hiding
Grandmother will keep my grinning cheeky face in a box,
my small-limbed body alive, and expect me to stay this way.
She will do this for her daughter too.

Rakaya Fetuga

Personal Apocalypse

I

when turbulence is your nursery rhyme
a plague is light work.
when the world fell apart
she said she was making tea
waiting for the oven to scorch toxins off her chicken thigh.
I'm doing alright, just fighting with the Council
she'd made it out of the suffocating house
indifferent to the air outside, soiled with smog
and arrived at a tight, windowless studio
with piss stains on the wall.
when I try her recipe for chilli chicken with orange glaze
I catch sight of my neighbours from the kitchen window
burning themselves with panic
a dragon-roar judders out from a gaunt and gawky woman
still in her house slippers, she sets two boys alight
for playing ball games at a time like this.
whenever I call, my friend is making tea.
just wait, it's never the first time
the world has ended

II

How to Read the Poem Before

A kitchen scene. Warm light, suggesting sunset or inferno.
POET enters, stage left, and massages new colour into raw, chicken flesh.

When POET speaks, there is glass in their voice: thick, cool-touch, and always at risk
of shattering. Glass separates POET from the nameless neighbours
whose stories are narrated to us from a distance. POET is inside, watching the fire,

and trying to hold flames down in a gut spitting acid –
POET *shows the remnants of this in every seventh word,*
or just enough to crack through the smoothed cement of monotone.
Remember, there is danger both outside the house and in.

Rip

After Kim Addonizio

And then there was the man who shoved me back from his taxi door,
a hand on my stomach, saying 'only two' could ride to Ains Khef
that much I understood; his foreign touch translating to:
you have been chosen as the disposable cargo,
until my host, reprimanding in Derija, convinced him
that three could fit in his five-seater car.
Had I been another me, I would have stalked away, hailed a new driver
and covered the old in a skid-cloud of sand
but my host nodded,
his head, a clicking lock.
I got in, trying not to see the driver's eyes in the rear-view mirror
or the reflection of all my heavy, dark skin –
instead, I found in the back of the driver's seat, a ripped hole
shaped like an overripe mango smashed on the floor
like the ones in my grandma's garden in Accra that April,
which, sweltering and trampled by wedding guests,
littered the earth yellow and green,
their sweet gumminess filling the air
while my American cousin,
afraid to touch his miniature flip-flops to the sticky ground,
wailed 'I don't like these mangoes!'
a phrase we still invoke for a cheap laugh,
although he is taller than me now and will never be cradled
in his father's arms again as he was on grandma's compound.
At her funeral, we all posed for a photo in matching black and white cloth
an 'uncle' (not in the family fabric) stood by me, smiling,
his hand reaching over my shoulder to cup my budding breast
while I stared deep into the camera lens, unmoving.
We jolt in the Moroccan man's taxi with no seatbelts,

a silent ride for a fermenting afternoon
his head wobbling into view with the tremor of rotten fruit
before the drop and smash to gasping earth.

Rosanna Hildyard

Half Empty

You say: *it covers too much*
when I say
I like your beard.

A tombstone shrug when
I suggest a walk
you've been there before.

Phone light shining on
your face: my personal
definition of blue.

The air between us
a distorted body
on the mattress.

I meter out affection
in small change. Clink. Clank.
A pocket half-full.

Things that remind me
of this: holding a glass of water
brimming over,

a smooth egg cracking in
my big baby fist, walking past
the green screens inside PaddyPower

seeing loosed wild horses,
the jockey
whipping. Clinging on.

You can have something
and still want it.
You can have something

Questions
are a halved
speech. Your jaw

a pale semicircle.
I fill a cup. Drink.
When will you leave me?

When your body no longer belongs to you

symptoms include feeling weak   this is not meant to be a criticism
        take a seat and help yourself to tea   no I'm sorry I was being annoying

I've taken a sleeping pill and I think it's still inside me
        I'm on my way to the high street will you meet me in a café?
I love those iron supplements they taste of strawberries

you're ruining your life it's selfish   go on lend us a tenner for a latte and a Danish
of all the cells in the human body they are the largest
                please tell me how you first noticed the
                sweating a test gone wrong

symptoms include hunger   you have to go to hospital right now you could have a seizure
                some faceless cluster growing inside
    it's seventy-five per cent all will be fine

under a microscope they look like tiny glowing suns   you've got very small veins do you have someone
the ultrasound shows nothing untoward   that guy you liked, is he still here?

I don't even want to see you I just phoned to vent

my mother came down we had falafel and then she went

the options are medical or surgical treatment or removal so I said I want to be on my own

from the moment you are born everything you'll be is packed inside   you're young and healthy otherwise

we'll wait a week month year and then we'll check again

the doctors don't know why these things happen

it comes from the Latin meaning *to swell*

it's natural for living things to want to grow

this soil is good for nothing but weeds   it was a brand-new house but the rot had set in

that man's got a tattoo of stitches on his head   it is lucky lucky lucky to have a body keeping nothing but you alive

she's allowed to drink now and her stomach's gone down   we're doing a magnolia walk while the sun's out

this is what you don't have but I enclose a leaflet   and for the rest of your life we'll check again

and anyway   the voices have been slowing recently

I got on my bike

felt that rush of blood between my legs again

Minying Huang

Arrangements Around the Fact

History now appearing before us tessellated, its polygonal dimensions cleanly contortions protruding from the insides of ellipses stretched beyond the topological assumption. Skin jerked beyond recognition, no rounding the corner, we hit it sharply head on, losing the sense of it. *There*. There is the dark we cannot see. Folded away, its excesses unsettled in the thick and thicket of all our beginnings, middles, and ends, crowding the eye for miles on end. Already collapsed, collapsing, in on itself. Accounting for the localised minutiae, a novel mess, too many turns away from narrative arching its back to touch every part of the whole, so wholly impossible, yet here, here we are so impossibly swept up in its yearning.

Second Impression

In the open air, a looseness of light. Its murmuration across the damp drag
of cornea over a cloud sea of faces, of heels until heaven—a sleight
of perception turning its hand through the eye, my mind to you, as scattered as light
in the open air. Gathered before me: congregation of cloth; burnish, billow,
tumble of hair; shadows caught lost in the lap of your creases, incisive strokes of
genius where you arch your brow, cock your mouth; optic gleam, lustre spreading open
the hours, *and in the brash I think I could love you.* A rush of blood to the head.
We stand dishevelled, you by the wind. I am contemplating the quirk of your neck,
sly of your fingertips, tug of your lip, *I wish you would*—and thereafter in the
blinking of seconds, my notion of us against time, its serrations of hue bent
into the singular: blur of many; sympathetic vibration in and of
skirmish of colour. Flooding the iris, you disassemble me, and is there no
gradation of light that would move you to compose me? In the open air—the way
a looseness of light becomes you, scintillating—our shoulders brushed against the grain.

Gabriel Jones

Did You Hear Last Week, Mum, When You Spoke and the Flowers Grew?

How you were closing the window, turned, said, *Dad seems
really pale*. How next door, the builders had left wet clay clustered
on the bed, hoist, table, floor. Sticky cold clods roughing over
the edges, how the ceiling bulb had drawn into itself, shivering.
How I found a lone monk in a wheelchair plastered in my head.

How I started moving in slow motion, like when I was Neil Armstrong
in the year 5 school play, stepping out of a cardboard rocket, trying
to leave even footprints in the sludge. Did you feel how we balanced
Dad's body? Hands under his armpits, our stomachs sucked, how I clanged
the wheelchair, footrest against the frame, his hearing aid swearing,

the air briefly metallic. How we held him aloft, just long enough
to release him, unfolded his neck into the pillow. Did you see
how he watched my hushed touch, my pottery eyes? Interested, maybe,
to see if cracks appeared. How you put a wrist to your forehead, said   *wow
    I'm tired.*   How then, a crack, finally, spidered.

Did you notice the magenta and purple flowers twisting headfirst, silent
umbrellas pushing through the crevice, flopping off their damp cladding,
emerald leaf tips bouncing into the centre of the room, shrugging
of course we're here. Did you see me seeing you? Fresh light filtering
onto your cheeks. How Dad, beaming, watered each of us in turn.

Underground

After a conversation with Chris Petts

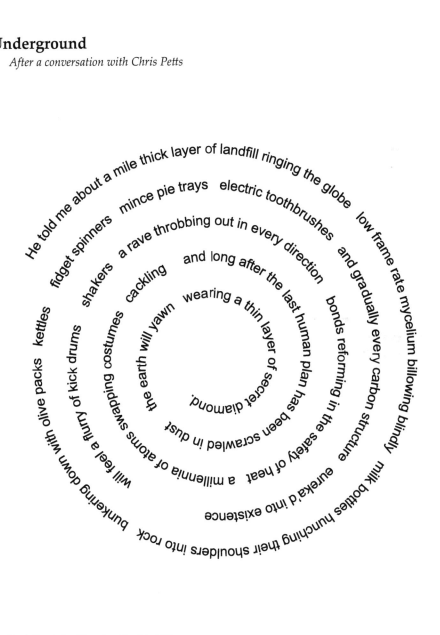

He told me about a mile thick layer of landfill ringing the globe low frame rate mycelium billowing blindly milk bottles hunching their shoulders into rock bunkering down with olive packs kettles fidget spinners mince pie trays electric toothbrushes and gradually every carbon structure bonds reforming in the safety of heat eureka'd into existence a millennia of atoms swapping costumes shakers a rave throbbing out in every direction and long after the last human plan has been scrawled in dust wearing a thin layer of secret diamond. the earth will yawn cackling will feel a flurry of kick drums

Kerrica Kendall

Balloos

After Camilla Anvar

I don't talk balls
I don't do fallacies
they float along to noodles

I don't talk balls
I don't do fallacies
they don't float along to noodles

I don't tock balls
ey don't do fallacies
they know float along to noodles
BANG! cash loose tit tots in locks for lucks pro-frolicks for fucks pro bucks
my nucks hurt, MUM!

(playful) !Torpeeeedoes! *(loving)* doesn't KNOW the WAY of my LIFE!
(surprised) BANG! let loose, forge boots ahead of TIME!
(surprised) BANG! tight new knoots to recover to wild what's ot Mine I spoke to liver to river to
dinner to singer to linens to binmens to freshmins to count its the blue tits to noon to to bang to the
river, *(slowly)* to my liver *shine!* where I am making wine. For dinner.

bang!

bang!

On Monday, I cooked up pasta sauce I called vomit. I fried diced onion, a cracked carrot, then garlic, in olive oil. I waited. Not too long. Meanwhile, heat up soy milk in a mug until it's lukewarm – if you want to – sometimes it forms a uh *(begins to shout)* sometimes it forms a goo, so, so watch out!

Friend: Listen, it's okay not to know.
(okay)

(right side look) They look so weird.
(left side look) I don't care. Screw you sideways.
(look centrally) I do care - don't go back now. Just. Carry on wearing it.
(right side look with disgust)
(shouting) I'm actually really stupid!

Do do, do do
Do do, do do
Do do do do, do do
You could drive a person crazy
You could drive a person mad*
Do do do do do do do do do do do do do do do do do do do do...

---

*   From You Could Drive a Person Crazy by Stephen Sondheim

F

bit a bank of frozen banana.
made two notes too musical. Two
strings, of banana, gone bonkers, conducting:

f for feeling underwhelmed rightnowy

my brain sunk into some pool above my nose or neck, my belly sucks,
set out a decking for not much, stewed my family for two years,
did a lot of forgiving I didn't want to do, accrued debt, broke the back of the decks, chairs,
f for loving the sound of the sound of belly tied, beaten. Eggs. Chairs.
Eggs. Eggs. Eggs. Eggs. Eggs. Eggs. Eggs. Eggs. Eggs. I just make eggs.
Splintered. Forced. Eggs to the whisk. Beat it. Found. Air trapped in eggs.
Mapped. I lost the yolk. Blinked. Burnt in sleep. Cartoned. Soy. Benign.

Rachel Lewis

Did I Watch You Kill a Lake Monster?

Did I watch you kill a lake monster with a tail thicker than your body,

did I applaud you, and did you give me an amphibian grin

while rain streaked our windows like children's fingers smearing aquarium glass

and did my hand on your shoulder feel like a fork breaking skin

and did my touch swallow conversation like the lake downing dead catch

and did that evening box us up like leftovers

and did we sit inside tupperwares,

bowl-eyed, separately portioned, chilled to our fillets?

Or did you give me a controller, make me your player 2,

and did I help you butcher the enormous fish,

did we load up your inventory with jewels

prised from unearthly salamander eyes,

and did you sell our winnings to the merchant,

buy a harpoon upgrade, skewer me on the shore?

Yahrzeit

A tuxedo cat is no husband.
All unmarried people are in hell, actually,
with soul guts flapping
and half a face –

don't roll your eyes,
isn't this what you're for?
Use a bone pen
split like a delicate hoof.

Use your office chair for kindling,
offer me winter roses
lined with diamante frost –
look at you, eyes fastened on a song.

How did your fields die?
You're not a farmer?
Your knuckles are peeling open,
how painful that must be,

saggy nerves hanging out.
I notice cherries on the counter,
yellow sleet and black-backed gulls.
I need two silver coins for my return.

My ashes tickle me,
I'm fraying at the toes,
the wise ones have passed on
but I think I can help.

There shines my poor brother,
his white and oily dumpling face.
Let him in too,
our mother tongue is balding.

My will and testament declare
one day we'll fill the garden with our talk.
Sleep now, I'll patch your skin,
leave the light on for me.

Cia Mangat

Backstroke

Consider the life of Princess Diana for a moment.
Princess Diana's birthday was in July,
which makes her a Cancer. The human body
is around 65% water, but Princess Diana's
body contained significantly more, because
she was a Cancer & had a tumultuous
personal life. Inside Princess Diana's silk shirts
& shoulder padded blazers her heart sloshed
around, but no one ever listened closely enough
to hear over the noise of the camera shutters.
Once, she visited a woman in hospital who leant
her head on the Princess' chest - mainly for the photos –
& told her nurse that night that she could hear something
splashing in there. Like kids at a community
swimming pool. Or like sparkling objects
encountering one another in water, sapphires
and ice cubes clinking at a party in everyone's drinks.
Her nurse didn't believe her. It's difficult having a heart
as blue as that. You get breathless up the stairs,
you find yourself jealous of the baby on the bus,
lying on its back, reaching for the top of its buggy.
Your heart needs central heating in December
so you consider strapping a hot water bottle to your
chest, but that feels too much like guarding a secret.
Princess Diana was too beautiful not to have secrets.
She dreamt of crown jewels sinking to the bottom
of the pool & how the water shot up her nose
& into her brain if she tried to reach for them.
After Princess Diana died an FOI revealed that
over 1000 pages of data had been accumulated

by the National Security Agency that organised
them in a filing cabinet, which was not waterproof.
Princess Diana's favourite way of swimming
was on her back, because she was a Cancer
& she knew that someone was always watching.

Special Effects

and then there was the august you found yourself
passed out on the floor of the hairdresser's

because it was the hottest summer on record and you hadn't drunk
enough water, and afterwards everyone said your body folded into itself

like collapsible idea furniture trying to disappear. still you keep finding yourself reduced
to a pile of clothes on your bed, a stack of bandages

in the chair of the blood test clinic - is it true that once you even managed to fold
yourself into such neat corners in the heat of the bazaar in your ma's hometown

that the man behind the counter selling her cheap bedsheets
initially mistook you for one of his cushions and sat you down

in a chair, asking one of his boys to bring a bottle of limca as a reward for the woman
whose daughter could evacuate herself so quickly that

those boys now swear when their bodies disappear
their hair will be what leaves first?

Sarah McCreadie

A Personal Definition of Light or Things that Light Up the Dark

There is a certain light in every McDonald's, greasy salt fingers cast in egg yolk sunburst yellow, it is warm in there, and running cold water over wrists, washing the good time off with the Pepto Bismol soap gunk when you slow dance with the soap dispenser that makes you sticky once more, sticky like when you cut a mango with plastic cutlery or like Year 9 biology. What about the laugh in the static at the end of a phone line or the bottle of nail polish that I thought looked like lilac curdled milk. Calon Lan sang by a grandmother. Twenty-four hours of news or supermarkets or breathing. That dogs shake their happy hips. That whistles will blow at three o'clock on a Saturday. That I am able to snap my back and stand up straight in a city and that there are things people will still queue for. The cowslip growing in the carpark. To ask a stranger the time and the relief it hasn't stopped.

Sweat on the Punch Bag, 1987

He is teenaged and weighed down by it all
By the rocks in his boxing gloves
And his heavy, shy eyes
They can't afford to turn the lights on in the hall
The boys spar and jab in the afternoon grey

He is permitted to see the other boys' bodies
When they swing and puncture the clouds of cigarette smoke
Believes the song on the radio says to him
A vision of love wearing boxing gloves, singing hearts and flowers
And with the feeling he gets
With a twist of the neck
Towards the dancing white vests
And tightly-strung shoes
Well, how could anyone tell him he is wrong

Shanay Neusum-James

Sovereign Blues

I love cigarettes
like my mum,
don't feel bad
when I'm doing her proud,
I used to beg her to stop,
I'm okay, I have
a dad in Catford,
I'm excited to drink,
I love sex in theory,
pretend my pillow is a boyfriend,
the arguments are never that bad,
it's so easy to make up
when you are already in bed.
I rehearse my proposal reaction
especially the pause
the before yes.
I have decided
I do,
I have to say yes.
I remember all the people
who have called me good girl,
I'm so nasty,
I don't believe my body,
I pop my spots
all over the world

Tasmia

I Am No Gold Star Dyke by Any Means

but an ode to the women who live long under my skin.

a moment please for the willowy firebrand I meet in
boutique bathroom chic, edible elation softening
any shame that might have lingered for
my graceless gait,
for the makeup scattered clumsily into the sink. I
bite back filth,
puddling under your steady scrutiny.
eventually leave, a number inscribed to memory,
dignity barely intact.
hallelujah!
our whirlwind affair ensues, flush with us
forgetting how to be morning people,
frittering away twilight hours, mapping
new ways to scale each other's   heights.

one day, I am crossing   the street to Hakeem's and you call
as you step into the shower.   the heavens crescendo
as i watch,
dumbfounded.
unconcerned with the cacophony of cusses
raining down as you bring me stumbling
  to my knees *again,* *again* *and again.*

Your Baba, Gentle Giant with Big Hands and Porous Heart

wears Ralph Lauren charity shop cuts with pride,
  and loves: a) his wife, b) his kids, in that order.
proclaims to the Uber driver 'I too have *THREE* daughters'
chest puffed plump robin, his big hand squeezes yours
  with too much force. flexing second-degree scald,
casualties birthed in curry house kitchen flames.
   once, they say, as a construction worker in Saudi,
baba saved a man's life, how he pulled a man clean out
   from under a building crumbling to dust.
still, your baba who could not pass jagged glass
  on the street without plucking it out of harm's way
wiggles nicotine-stained fingers, winces only *once,*
   assures you: 'it *barely* hurts'

Maeve Slattery

May You Love in Ways Which Disrupt State Violence

Begin again – 14th June 2017. A tower in West London is on fire with people inside. 8am, those trapped are most definitely dead. Nearby, children pick through donations scattered across church floors, left with love by a dawn chorus. They're the opposite of vultures, cautiously hopping from side to side. As the day's light fades, parents notice t-shirts blossom with missing faces. Months later, these children still reach to hold their friends.

Begin again – 9:30am, 14th June. What you long for is knowing. Alicia walks home but where does she live? You return grateful, a week later, to sitting in a room with her saying, *Yesterday I went to the shops and bought...* She magics riches: Gucci sliders, unlimited slime.

Begin again – seal donations, so mice don't get in. Repeatedly packing boxes is a distraction. Skip to Grenfell Inquiry revelations in 2020. Peter Maddison tries to hide notebooks under his bed. Claire Williams admits to binning hers in 2018. People with authority get paid to shred other people's traces.

Begin again – the 2019 Stability Index report found that 45,000 looked-after children had their social worker change at least once between 2017 and 2018. More than 20,000 – just over 1 in 4 – dealt with 2 or more changes in that time. Children like Alicia, face a change in their worker as the main source of disruption in their lives.

Begin again – 2021. A London council sells off its Leaving Care building during COVID. Kareem volunteers to bring the new office to life. His favourite flower is lavender, he collages with seeds. Workers scheme ways to ask big bosses to make things safe with any urgency: say, young people need fresh air – this kitchen has no windows that open; say, we only need a section of the garden; say, we can look after our people ourselves.

Begin again – being a person, not composed of grand gestures.

Since Things Are Uncertain

Consider marigolds.
Marigolds can be orange, yellow or red
and are often referred to as calendula.
Like all flowers,
they're at risk of pesticides and piss.
Still, they have medicinal purposes.
Their vibrant petals are coloured by lutein
and deep green leaves, zeaxanthin.
Both protect against overly bright light,
including blue UV.

Marigold oil can be eaten by the spoonful,
drizzled on salads, rubbed into hands.
Infuse petals with a carrier oil, such as olive.
Over time, it'll turn a dark orange or even red.

Every marigold loses its petals.
What remains is a green clenched fist,
made up of small thin moons.
Each moon is a seed, creating hundreds
if not thousands of new moons.
Wait until the moons turn dry brown.

Marigolds almost always grow.
They flower in winter, survive harsh winds.
This is why they're my most consistent teachers.
I used to be so scared of killing life,
I couldn't grow anything.
Now I let out the agitated air to a flat surface.
I have new tools to notice unexpected gifts.

Matt L T Smith

When Light Seeps In

Slicing through her belly, curtains cracked apart.
I didn't hear blood beating at the window.
If you keep the curtains closed it's never raining.
I watch morning drain from her face. How unwieldy is sunlight?
It hits me like a memory untempered by dreams: birth is a blade.

Slicing through   curtains

I watch morning   wield   sunlight
        like a   tempered   blade

Infuse Me with a Black Hole to Keep the Light In

My spine bleeding, lightning buzzing in the small of my back.
She pulls the blue curtains around me, her mouth a closed wound,
red fills my chest, the first time I've ever seen heartbreak on skin.
White spots on my MRI. A tower block at 3am with a few restless owls
awake in squares of light, soulful dreamers escaping the confines of night.

My spine bleeding light
    pull the   curtains   a closed wound

a   soul   escaping

I'm convinced people only exist inside boxes of light.
How many disembodied friends' faces have I held in my palm?
I no longer have evidence they exist anywhere else, just
the softness of their radiance, the warmth of a phone on my cheek. Can I
keep them? A belonging, contained forever in a cube of light. Always in touch.

      a   face   in my palm

the softness of   a   warm   cheek
     A   longing   for   touch

Without asking, a nurse readjusts my mask for me. Did I always recoil
at intimacy? How isn't this gravity keeping the light in? But it bends the nose
of my neurologist's mask until it drops, gifts a glance at her kind face.
She brings it to her mouth, jots down the risky meds I ask for, taps on my face,
asks if I can feel it. I ask her to keep tomorrow waiting. Stop the light draining.

     How   gravity   bends

  brings   down the sky   on my face
          to keep   the light   in

Simran Uppal

Recipe Prayer for a Fridge Full of Tupperware

1. Keep garlic and ginger in the freezer.[1]
2. Fry them with jeera till it's right.[2]
3. Add haldi, garam masala, chilli.[3]
4. Add baked beans, or whatever you have.[4]
5. Serve it with rice, and achar.[5]
6. Toast is OK, or whatever you have.[6]
7. My friend's Mum cooked karela for me, and two kinds of rice.[7]
8. You have to salt it for hours, then it feeds you for days.[8]

My Dadi ate gobi for weeks so her kids could have more.
Nani-ma got locked out her country for 40 years,
but cooked us cold noodles with lime, fish sauce, fried garlic.
My Mum doesn't like to cook: Nani-ma cooked
while her husband drank, and shouted. When I go to Mum's, I cook.
She watches, excited: fish sauce, sabjis, dishes and dishes of rice.

1   Mom preps it herself, a day a month, blender full of garlic, kitchen air raw and delicious. I buy it from Iceland, important as eggs.

2   Cumin. Mum made me smell the jar then the air above the spattering oil - suddenly nutty, like gold should smell.

3   Tumeric. You shouldn't be able to smell it. Mum says the flavour is bad - you add it for colour, and health. I hate when white people look all eager and tell me how they love the taste. I don't care.

4   Dadi-ji did it with baked beans, but my Nani, Mum's mum, did it with tins of fish. The same - when there's no food in the fridge, or guests come by, so you give them all you cooked.

5   Imagine: No rice? You didn't put it on already? That's OK, Simran darling.

6   My Mum makes darling a suffix, like Simran-darling is one word. You can call someone 'jaan', my soul, my life, or you can add it to their name. Amma-jaan: Mum, my own life.

7   Bitter gourd. I used to hate it, but it's good for your blood, and good with lime, fish sauce, rice. My Mum's side lived in Burma for years: she has these three with everything, and fresh coriander.

8   My Dadi packed us boxes of dal whenever we left her house. When Mum was pregnant with me the nausea was bad, so Dadi-ji made her special parathas with ajwain, sweet bitter seeds for her tummy, and hid them in the middle of the stack so no one else would eat them.

Poppers

work when you give head too. I keep my bottle
in my socks with my card, like everyone else.
Vault on Thursday is *Stripped*: no clothes,
no pockets, so busy you can barely move.
Someone in the darkroom holds my back.
He kisses me. Soon I'm breathing molten plastic,
sharp wine. Forget your breath. No arms, no legs,
no kneeling, throat slick, wide. Float—

     They're playing a techno remix of Toxic. Forget to breathe.
     Dark spots in eyes, tightness, tight—   push away.

        I'm at a sauna, after, with a boy I used to kiss at clubs.
        It's free for under 25s tonight. Old men rush over
        pushy, try to join when I stop kissing and
        drop down. I open the poppers bottle that was tucked
        in his towel and smile up. I lean in, breathe. Float in.
        I rest my forehead against his hip.

Maggie Wang

In Gratitude
after Abigail Carroll

for the circumflex, the open mouth,
the yawn of a stranger's half-spoken
last wish, the chasm across which

the season's first climbers string
their lines without hesitating; for
orthographic kidnappings and the way

you memorialize them each time
you sign your name, a sigh across
the wide round stomach of okeanos

where *magnificat anima mea*
dominum et exultavit spiritus meus;
for the mornings when you wake to

birdsong in the shape of your family
tree, take your language and lay it
against my forehead, a blessing

so that I might better understand you,
so that I might confess to you in your
mother tongue that I love you; for

the opening that would follow,
the pause in your breathing between
one word and the next, the suspension

of time between lightning and thunder;
for the empty space in a medieval
manuscript left for illuminators who

never arrived, the folds in the vellum
glossed by the tired monk's pen
beneath which the alphabet that made

your life possible is born; and for
you, who alone would brave with me
the unknowable, unpronounceable waves.

Summer Slept Buried

in a pit of pine needles,
and the quart of pond water trapped by her heat
did not evaporate like the soft august sky,
which took with it your memory of how the stars
looked in the hemisphere of your birth.
from where you lay, the wool of your sleeves
melted back into the skin of its shearing,
on which a scribe whose name is lost to history
once spent his life writing around the edges,
the oil of his fingertips placating the parchment
like the weight of god's hand on your shoulder.
no matter how slowly it happened,
you were always naked by the end, shivering
on the brutalist deck of the next crossing
downstream, where ice climbed like barnacles
from the footing. when in doubt, you reminded
yourself that this was how the sheep felt
afterwards, stomachs inscribed by the insouciant
grass with a prayer for the kind of oblivion
that is merciful, its rhythms halting bilingual
like the silent tongues of an ancient stele.

Jinhao Xie

Consequences of Learning a New Language

I am most at home   when the wall
of my stomach   collapses

my tongue   acidic   eroded
          bites   the bullet-sized grains
                    of alphabets   like the first time
I was stung   by a singing jellyfish

ask me how much I love you   ask me how deep I do
just go to your window   and find my love
in the shape   of a ghost moon

she morphs nostalgia
croissants   dried mango   red bean paste

          I arrive with my body   brass & fluid
          my sorrow has encrusted to this new accent

the next second   a stretched-out   sentence
I dream of   a crudely smudged embryo
shelled   by a staircase
                              my body
wants to leave   in fact   to be left behind
the ones I truly loved   we understand each other
without pronouns and articulations

our promise   a pinky swear
& two thumbs' kiss
like fish   hope is seaweed
roped around my waist

Hotpot is All/That We Can Talk About/
While Watching Eat Drink Man Woman

instead the film opens/with us diving
in/to a babbling pot/our foreheads/threads
of sweat-pearls/a chandelier/of condensation/
above our dining table/one naked light-
bulb drips/from the ceiling/lilting/our shadows/a shrine
of buddha/my grandmother sits with us/so still/she sits
in her obituary photograph/*I try to remember her*/mother tilts
her head/unfolds her eyelids/as if recalling yesterday's
news/*as if she was listening*/*and she listens*, I say

she listens.

1999, New Year's Eve/we are terrible
actors/no audience/to convince/no red lanterns/only our
roasted cheeks/festive words/everyday
bowls and chopsticks/*don't drum*
the bowl/don't kick underneath the table back and forth/
mother shouts waving two sticks/*you are kicking*
your ancestors/stop eating with your left hand/stop
fighting with your brother/why do you ask so many
questions? /why aren't you like other kids?

and they forget to write my father/any words/
he/a mannequin, posing/we don't speak to him/just
between us/understand that he prefers cigarettes
mixed with rice/his face, pixelated/*it's an aesthetic choice*
they say/self-satisfied/ I cry, *it's not fair* /as it's written
in the script/then an outburst of laughter/*you*

are just a kid/they mock/*you won't remember/any*
of this/so I kick/and I kick/
with my bare feet/run to my grandmother's
grave/waking her/from her dream/and I scream

didn't you hear me?!

the director instructs my mother/to blow away the halo
steaming off her face/her spiced lips/red
chillies afloat/in the broth/turquoise crabs and moon-lit
prawns/scratching/for salvation/as they are set free
from the silver lining/of a dollar shop
platter/their bodies/perfectly cooked amber gems/we find
from the valley of the pot/*I hope*
they had their own gods, brother says, *to pray a new life*
like ours/eat eateat eat, mother tuts with chopsticks, hitting
the rim of our bowls/*loads of nonsense/your grandma*
never had our 口福/*don't spoil your chance*

the roofs/of our mouths/heavens

because budget permits/they want drama and conflicts/
ask us to swallow whole moons/of octopus/our heavens/burn
as we recite our words/*what's the hurry* mother pants/ and I say
nothing/brother sits/faceless/neck-twisted to the balcony
window/watching fireworks/and then
he grabs me/by the left hand/like his beloved toy soldier/and we run
downstairs/knocking on our neighbours' doors/*happy*
new year! happy new year! happy new year! happy new…/trailing behind/our mother
screeching in her pink plastic flipflops/our father
a man-sized cardboard/inside an open casket/of our window
look! we point/and then,
the countdown begins/and we
step back/into 轟鬧的night/our flat/aflame
/and our inflammable father
diminishes into a sigh/of birthday candles/and the shuttle
stutters/we make a wish

Biographies

Oshanti Ahmed [9]
Oshanti Ahmed is a Bengali poet by the way of South London. She is an alumnus of the Roundhouse Poetry Collective, and Apples and Snakes' The Writing Room. She was longlisted for the Out-Spoken Prize for Poetry 2020 (Page Poetry) and a Roundhouse Slam finalist 2020. Her work has been featured on the FADER and BBC Radio 4 and she has performed both nationally and internationally including at Brave New Voices, Brainchild Festival, Latitude Festival and The Haye Festival.

Esme Allman [21]
Esme Allman is a poet, writer, theatre-maker, and facilitator based in South-east London. She works in a multi-disciplinary way exploring blackness, desire, imagination, and the intersection of these themes. Esme's work has appeared at the Barbican Centre, English Heritage and the ICA, BBC Radio 3, and BBC Radio 6. Most recently, she was awarded an Artist Residency at the Roundhouse in performing arts for the year 2021/2022.

mandisa apena [22]
mandisa apena is a cancer sun from South London. they are an interdisciplinary artist interested in herbalism, dreams, and nature worship. they have a self-published poetry book called 'and twice as bitter' (2016), and have been described as 'hilarious' and 'interesting.'

Rachel Cleverly [19]
Rachel Cleverly is a poet and producer. She is an Old Vic Theatre Maker and an alumnus of Apples and Snakes' The Writing Room and BBC Words First. She has an MA in Creative Writing from the University of East Anglia and has been published by SPAM, ACHE Magazine, The Feminist Library, Ink, Sweat & Tears, and Black Sunflowers Press among others. Rachel works as an Education Officer at The Poetry Society, where she manages the Foyle Young Poets of the Year Award.

Bella Cox [1]
An internationally acclaimed multi-disciplinary artist, Bella Cox has worked for over 6 years as a poet, workshop facilitator, MC, and event producer in Kenya, South Africa, and

the UK. She is a twice-nominated young people's laureate, and was a member of multiple poetry collectives throughout 2018.

Her art spans the disciplines of poetry, prose, music, theatre, and crafting. She is well-known for pieces that address the notions of home, belonging, and identity, as well as for her proudly queer and feminist work that seeks to embrace difference and empower others. Her performances often involve a loop pedal which she uses with her voice to create intricate soundscapes underscoring her poems. Bella is currently working on her debut poetry pamphlet to be released with flipped eye publishing in 2022.

Courtney Conrad [18]

Courtney Conrad is a Jamaican poet. Her poetry explores themes of migration, religion, and womanhood. She is a member of The London Library Emerging Writers Programme, and Malika's Poetry Kitchen. An alumnus of Obsidian Foundation and Roundhouse Poetry Collective. A Bridport Prize Young Writers Award recipient shortlisted for The White Review Poet's Prize and Oxford Brookes International Poetry Competition and longlisted for the Rebecca Swift Women Poets' Prize. Her poems have appeared in Magma Poetry, Poetry Wales, The White Review, Stand Magazine, bath magg and Poetry Birmingham Literary Journal. She has performed at festivals including Glastonbury Festival, Brainchild Festival and UKYA City Takeover.

Geraint Ellis [2]

Geraint Ellis is a Northumbrian-Welsh poet, living in London. He is a former Scottish National Slam Poetry finalist and has written extensively for comedy programmes on BBC Radio 4. He has produced radio programmes for the BBC, Absolute Radio, XFM and Capital. He is currently writing his first collection.

Abena Essah [13]

Abena Essah is a poet, musician and creative of many hats based in London. Their practice often explores the intersections of their queer identity, Ghanaian heritage and reimagining/decolonising the lens with which black history is told.

Abena has been published by Spread the Word, with Ink Sweat and Tears, South London Gallery, and Marques Almeida for London Fashion Week 2020. They are also an alumnus of the Obsidian Foundation and Apples and Snakes' The Writing Room and the Roundhouse Poetry Collective. Currently,they are a Roundhouse Resident Artist.

Rakaya Fetuga [14]

Rakaya Fetuga is a writer from North-West London of Ghanaian and Nigerian heritage. Rakaya is a former Roundhouse Resident Artist (2019-21), winner of the Roundhouse Poetry Slam (2018) and Rooftop Rhythms x Brooklyn Poetry Slam (2020), as well as being twice shortlisted for the Out-Spoken Prize for Poetry (2018/2019). Rakaya's commissions and partnerships include work for the UNFPA, BBC, Bloomberg Philanthropies x Vanity Fair, and Apple. Rakaya is a regular workshop facilitator for the Poetry Society and hosts the Rumi's Cave Open Mic in North-West London. Rakaya has a Creative Writing MA from Royal Holloway, University of London, and is working on her first novel.

Rosanna Hildyard [15]

Rosanna Hildyard is an editor and writer from North Yorkshire. She is an alumnus of the Roundhouse Poetry Collective. Her poetry and fiction has recently been published in Vittles, PERVERSE, Banshee and Modern Poetry in Translation, been shortlisted for the Benedict Kiely Award and come second in the Brick Lane Short Story Prize. Her short story collection, Slaughter, was longlisted for the Edge Hill Prize 2021 and is available from Broken Sleep Books.

Minying Huang [23]

Minying Huang is an Oxford-based poet. Their work appears in wildness, Palette Poetry, Electric Literature, and elsewhere. They are a doctoral student in the Faculty of Medieval and Modern Languages at the University of Oxford.

Gabriel Jones [5]

Gabriel is a multi-disciplinary artist from West Wales, working within poetry, theatre making and sound production. His work has appeared at the Albany, Barbican and Roundhouse, and on stages at Brainchild, Bestival and Lovebox. He was a BBC words first poet (2020) and a Roundhouse resident artist (2018) where he produced Let me out my room please; a collaborative poetry album, live show and pamphlet. He has been published in anthologies by Bad Betty and Mud Press. His writing is currently focused on family, mental health and what freedom means.

Kerrica Kendall [22]

Kerrica Kendall is a writer and performer. They are serious about silly, not-silly and having a very good time. They are also in the Bush Theatre Young Company & the National Film and Television School. Their first tiny play will be released this year.

Rachel Lewis [11]

Rachel Lewis is a poet and facilitator. She is interested in bringing attention to hidden pain, everyday joys, and love beyond romance. Her poetry interrogates and celebrates family, friendship, community, and recovery.

Her first pamphlet exploring eating disorder recovery, 'Three degrees of separation', was published in 2019 by Wordsmith HQ. She is currently writing a second collection exploring grief and belonging through her family's links to the Belfast Jewish community. Community is at the heart of her practice. She is a co-founder of the Writing Happiness Project supporting fellow D/deaf, disabled and neurodivergent writers @disabledjoy. She also runs a newsletter sharing free resources on the work of poetry.

Cia Mangat [12]
Cia Mangat is nineteen and from London. She is a Foyle Young Poet. At the moment, she studies English at uni, and edits Zindabad Zine.

Sarah McCreadie [16]
Sarah McCreadie is a poet, performer, and lesbian heartthrob from Cardiff, living in London. Sarah has performed her poetry from Newport to New York. She is a Barbican Young Poet, a BBC 1Xtra Words First poet, resident artist alumnus at the Roundhouse theatre and a former member of the Roundhouse's poetry collective. She has also collaborated with Vanity Fair, ITV, and The Guilty Feminist podcast.

Shanay Neusum-James [4]
Shanay Neusum-James is a writer and actress based in South-east London. She is an alumna of the Roundhouse Poetry Collective 19/21, Barbican Young Poets 21/22 and The Obsidian Foundation. Shanay has been published in Ambit Magazine, Magma and fourteenpoems journal. Her poem beside yourself was featured in Bradley Sharpe's debut collection 'BESIDE YOURSELF' at London Fashion Week 2021. Her debut pamphlet surrender dorothy is forthcoming with Bad Betty Press this year.

Tasmia [17]
Tasmia is a producer, writer and performer. They are an MFest Writers Lab alum and have previously been a writer in residence at the Nottingham Primary, performing on stages such as Latitude, Free Word Centre, and Rich Mix. Their writing explores relation, language memory, and the intricacies of imagining and manifesting possibilities from the margins. They also freelance as a trainer and an oral historian, currently archiving the history of Bengali seamstresses in East London during the 1970s.

Maeve Slattery [3]
Maeve Slattery is a poet, youth worker and programme manager from South London. She was longlisted for Culture Recordings' New Voice in Poetry Prize 2020. Maeve is interested in creativity as a form of witness, and approaches poetry, drawing and craft as trace, or evidence. Maeve runs poetry workshops for young people across London.

Matt L T Smith [6]

Matt L T Smith's poetry has appeared on BBC Radio 3 and Apples & Snakes' Blackbox series. His poem 'A Neurologist Flips a Coin into a Well' was recently commended in the Verve Poetry Competition. Matt works with people with dementia on the Finding the Words project with Anvil Arts, taking down conversations with participants and turning them into found poems.

Simran Uppal [10]

Simran (they/them) is a poet, yoga teacher, and community organiser based in East London. They're interested in translation, sensation, devotion, and the community body, particularly in the contexts of queer British Asian lives, London's cruising scenes, and unorthodox religious practices. Simran has written lyric essays, political journalism, and poems for The Independent, Burnt Roti, and the Consulate General of Italy, among others. Performances include work with The Isis, Raze Collective, Theater X in Berlin, and most recently at the Barbican Concert Hall.

Maggie Wang [7]

Maggie Wang's recent work appears in Evergreen Review, bath magg, and Poetry Wales. She is a Ledbury Emerging Poetry Critic and the reviews editor at SUSPECT, the journal of New York City-based-literary non-profit Singapore Unbound. She is especially interested in eco-poetics, multilingual poetry, and the intersections between poetry, history, and music.

Jinhao Xie [8]

Jinhao Xie, born in Chengdu, is a member of Southbank Centre New Poets Collective 2021-2022. Their work is in POETRY, Poetry Review, Harana, bath magg, Gutter Magazine, and anthologies, including Slam! You're Gonna Wanna Hear This, edited by Nikita Gill, Instagram Poems for Every Day by National Poetry Library, and Re.Creation (a forthcoming queer anthology). They are the inaugural champion of Asia House Poetry slam 2018. They are interested in nature, the mundane, the interpersonal and selfhood. They love to cook for their beloved.

Editors
Rachel Long
Jacob Sam-La Rose

Project Team
Artistic Director & Lead Facilitator Jacob Sam-La Rose
Co-Tutor Rachel Long
Creative Learning Producer (Theatre, Dance & Poetry) Lauren Brown

With thanks to:
Faith Austin
Tim Bifield
Lauren Monaghan-Pisano
Simon Morgan
Mariam Olaniyan
Natalie Omari
Rikky Onefeli
Matthew Turner
Paula Varjack

The Barbican is very grateful for the support of Julian Hale and Helen Likierman, of all our Patrons, Trusts and Foundations, Corporate Supporters, all the donors to the Barbican Fund and the many thousands who have made a donation when purchasing tickets.

Barbican Centre
Silk Street
London EC2Y 8DS

barbican.org.uk

Photographs by Betty Laura Zapata | www.bettylaurazapata.com; Christy Ku | www.christyku.co.uk; Robert Taylor | www.taylor-photo.co.uk

Interested in becoming a Barbican Young Poet?

Produce fresh, raw, and relevant work in the company of others who, like you, are passionately invested in the written and spoken word.

Barbican Young Poets is an artist development initiative and community for those who wish to explore what's possible for their poetry and creative expression. Through a six-month programme, you'll generate new writing, experiment with different ways of working, and refine a selection of your new work towards a publication and showcase. Barbican Young Poets is facilitated by internationally renowned poet and performer, Jacob Sam-La Rose, and co-tutor, Rachel Long, with special sessions from invited guest artists along the way.

See the Barbican website for further details, including when applications open.

Email creative.learning@barbican.org.uk to find out more.